24 Hours Inpiration

for a more productive and meaningful life

Tony Hendroyono

Table of contents

Happiness starts from the morning

Starting the day with positivity and a good mindset can set the tone for the rest of the day and lead to a happier and more productive experience. Research shows that having a morning routine that includes activities such as exercise, meditation, and goal-setting can help improve mood and overall well-being.

There have been several studies that have explored the impact of morning routines on mood and well-being. Here are a few examples:

- A study published in the Journal of Sleep Research found that people who woke up at consistent times and had established morning routines reported better moods and lower levels of stress compared to those who had more inconsistent sleep schedules.
- A study published in the Journal of Positive Psychology found that people who engaged in positive morning rituals, such as meditating or practicing gratitude, reported increased feelings of happiness and well-being throughout the day.
- Research published in the journal Personality and Individual Differences found that people who have established morning routines are better able to regulate their emotions, have greater feelings of control, and experience less stress throughout the day.
- Another study published in the Journal of Applied Psychology found that people who start their mornings with physical activity, such as exercise or yoga, reported improved moods and greater overall life satisfaction compared to those who did not engage in morning physical activity.

Early wake up in the morning also lead to greater prosperity, both in terms of personal and professional success. A successful and productive morning routine can help you prioritize your goals, focus your attention, and build momentum for the day ahead. Whether it's exercise, meditation, goal-setting, or simply taking time to plan out your day, the morning can be a powerful time for setting the stage for prosperity and success.

Many successful individuals are known for waking up early in the morning. Some examples include:

- Tim Cook, CEO of Apple, who wakes up at 3:45 am to start his day.
- Richard Branson, founder of the Virgin Group, who wakes up at 5:45 am and starts his day with exercise.
- Howard Schultz, former CEO of Starbucks, who wakes up at 4:30 am and uses the early hours for reading and reflection.
- Jack Dorsey, CEO of Twitter, who wakes up at 5:30 am and starts his day with meditation and exercise.
- Jeff Bezos, CEO of Amazon, who is known for waking up early to start his day with a clear mind and tackle tasks before distractions set in.

Early morning hath gold in its mouth.

BENJAMIN FRANKLIN

The early bird gets the worm.

Morning is an important time of day, because how you spend your morning can often tell you what kind of day you are going to have.

LEMONY SNICKET

The morning is a reminder that you
have another chance to be great.

UNKNOWN

Rise early, work hard, strike oil.

J. PAUL GETTY

Morning is wonderful. Its only drawback is that it comes at such an inconvenient time of day.

GLENCOOK

When you arise in the morning, think of what a precious privilege it is to be alive - to breathe, to think, to enjoy, to love.

MARCUS AURELIUS

An early-morning walk is a blessing
for the whole day.

HENRYDAVISTHOREAU

The morning is a great place to start
a new life.

The morning is the best time to start anew and to plan for a successful day.

UNKNOWN

The power of meditation

Starting the day with meditation can help you feel more calm, focused, and energized, allowing you to tackle the day's challenges with a clear mind and positive outlook.

Some of the most significant benefits of meditation include:

- Reduced Stress: Meditation can help reduce stress and anxiety levels by slowing down breathing and promoting relaxation.
- Improved Focus: Regular meditation can help improve focus and concentration, making it easier to stay on task and complete tasks efficiently.
- Increased Self-Awareness: Meditation can increase self-awareness, allowing you to understand your thoughts, feelings, and emotions more deeply.
- Better Sleep: Meditation can promote better sleep, helping you feel more refreshed and energized each day.
- Enhanced Mood: Regular meditation can improve mood and increase feelings of happiness, peace, and well-being.
- Boosted Immune System: Meditation has been shown to enhance the functioning of the immune system, helping to prevent illness and disease.
- Decreased Pain: Meditation can help reduce pain by lowering levels of stress hormones and increasing pain tolerance.

There are many successful figures who practice meditation, including:

- Oprah Winfrey: Oprah has been practicing meditation for decades and has credited it with helping her maintain balance and inner peace.
- Arianna Huffington: Huffington, the founder of the Huffington Post, is a passionate advocate for meditation and has written about its benefits for both personal and professional success.
- Steve Jobs: Jobs was known for his intense focus and drive, and he credited his regular meditation practice with helping him stay focused and calm in the face of challenges.
- Russell Simmons: Simmons, the co-founder of Def Jam Recordings, has been practicing meditation for over 30 years and has been an advocate for its benefits for both personal and professional success.
- Ray Dalio: Dalio, the founder of Bridgewater Associates, has been a long-time practitioner of meditation and has credited it with helping him stay focused and make better decisions in his professional life.

Meditation is the dissolution of thoughts in Eternal awareness or Pure consciousness without objectification, knowing without thinking, merging finitude in infinity.

S WAMI S I V AN AN D A

Meditation is not a way of making your mind quiet. It's a way of entering into the quiet that's already there.

DEEPAK CHOPRA

Meditation is not just a tool to calm the mind and reduce stress, but it's a method of self-discovery and liberation.

MATTHIEU RICARD

Meditation is the art of being still, of allowing the mind to come to a point of stillness so that the heart can open and the soul can shine through.

GABRIELLEBERNSTEIN

Meditation is a process of lightening up, of trusting the basic goodness of what we have and who we are, and of realizing that any wisdom that exists, exists in what we already have.

P E MA CH Ö D R Ö N

Meditation is the practice of training your mind to focus and redirect your thoughts, leading to increased awareness, calmness and inner peace.

ANONYMOUS

Meditation is a way for nourishing
and blossoming the divine within you.

AMI T R AY

Meditation is like a gym in which you develop the powerful mental muscles of calm and insight.

AJAH N B R AH M

A healthy mind in a healthy body

Many productive and successful people start their day with exercise because of the benefits it provides.

Exercising in the morning can offer several benefits, including:

- Improved mood: Exercise releases endorphins, the feel-good hormones, which can help improve your mood and reduce stress.
- Increased energy: Exercise gets your heart rate up, which can help boost your energy levels and improve mental alertness.
- Better focus: Exercise has been shown to improve cognitive function and increase focus, making it easier to tackle tasks throughout the day.
- Better sleep: Engaging in regular morning exercise can help regulate your circadian rhythm and improve the quality of your sleep.
- Better metabolism: Exercise in the morning has been shown to increase your metabolism, which can help you burn more calories throughout the day.
- Improved motivation: Starting your day with exercise can set a positive tone for the rest of the day, helping you stay motivated and focused.
- Increased accountability: By making exercise a regular part of your morning routine, you increase the chances of sticking with it and making it a habit.

Many successful people and leaders have been known to practice exercise in the morning as a means to boost their productivity and well-being. Here are a few examples:

- Tim Cook, CEO of Apple: Cook is known for starting his day with a 4:30 a.m. workout and has said that exercise helps him feel refreshed and energized.
- Oprah Winfrey: Oprah has been known to be an early riser and starts her day with a workout and meditation.
- Richard Branson, Founder of Virgin Group: Branson is known for his active lifestyle and is an advocate of starting the day with exercise, often sharing pictures of his early-morning kiteboarding sessions on social media.
- Barack Obama, Former President of the United States: Obama has been known to be an avid workout enthusiast and was known to start his day with a workout, often doing cardio and weightlifting.
- Jack Dorsey, CEO of Twitter: Dorsey is known for his early-morning routine and starts his day with a 6-mile run, meditation, and breakfast.

The morning is a fresh start to a new day, so make it count.

UNKNOWN

Early morning workout: destroyed yesterday's excuses.

UNKNOWN

Wake up, work out, repeat.

UNKNOWN

The morning is my favorite time of day because I feel like I have the world to myself.

Don't let yesterday take up too much of today.

WILLROGERS

It's not just about being fit, it's about feeling good and having the energy to live life to the fullest.

UNKNOWN

Start each day with a positive thought
and a grateful heart.

ROYBENNETT

The morning is a great opportunity to set the tone for the rest of the day. Make it count.

UNKNOWN

Exercise is the spark that ignites the
fire of wellness within you.

UNKNOWN

Sweat is magic. Cover yourself in it daily to grant your wishes.

Preparation is half of success

Preparation is a key factor in achieving success. By taking the time to properly plan and prepare, you can increase your chances of success by making sure that you have the necessary resources and knowledge to overcome potential obstacles and achieve your goals.

Preparation is crucial for having a productive day. Here are a few ways in which preparation can contribute to a productive day:

- Better time management: Preparation allows you to prioritize tasks, plan ahead, and manage your time effectively, which can lead to greater productivity and efficiency.
- Improved focus: By preparing for the day ahead, you can avoid distractions and stay focused on the tasks at hand.
- Reduced stress: Preparation helps you feel more in control of the day and reduces the stress of unexpected events or changes in plans.
- Better energy management: Preparing ahead of time can also help you manage your energy levels more effectively, allowing you to prioritize important tasks and avoid burnout.
- Increased motivation: Feeling prepared and organized can increase your motivation and drive to get things done.

Many successful people and leaders believe in the importance of preparation. Here are a few examples:

- Steve Jobs: The co-founder of Apple was known for his attention to detail and his commitment to preparation. He believed that preparation was key to success, and he spent countless hours preparing for product launches and presentations.
- Warren Buffett: The legendary investor and CEO of Berkshire Hathaway is known for his preparation and his ability to make informed decisions. He believes in taking the time to thoroughly research and understand a potential investment before making a decision.
- Barack Obama: The former President of the United States is known for his preparation and his ability to handle complex issues. He believes in being well-prepared for meetings, speeches, and negotiations, and his preparation has helped him effectively lead the country.
- Mark Zuckerberg: The CEO of Facebook is known for his preparation and his willingness to take calculated risks. He believes in preparing for the future by constantly learning and exploring new technologies, and his preparation has helped him build one of the world's largest technology companies.

By failing to prepare, you are
preparing to fail.

Proper preparation prevents poor performance.

UNKNOWN

Success is where preparation and opportunity meet.

BOBBY UNSER

If you fail to plan, you plan to fail.

ALAN LAKEIN

The more you sweat in peace, the less you bleed in war.

NORMAN SCHWARZKOPF

The future belongs to those who prepare for it today.

MAL CO L M X

The will to win is not nearly as important as the will to prepare to win.

BOBBYKNIGHT

Success is not final, failure is not fatal: it is the courage to continue that counts.

WINSTON CHURCHILL

Start the day with healthy food

Breakfast is considered to be one of the most important meals of the day, and for good reason.

Here are some of the key benefits of eating a nutritious breakfast:

- Provides energy: Breakfast provides the body with the energy it needs to start the day. Skipping breakfast can lead to fatigue, low energy levels, and decreased productivity.
- Boosts metabolism: Eating breakfast can help rev up your metabolism and jumpstart your body's natural fat-burning process.
- Supports healthy weight management: Studies have shown that people who eat breakfast regularly are less likely to be overweight or obese.
- Improves cognitive function: Breakfast provides the brain with the nutrients it needs to function properly, which can help improve focus, memory, and overall cognitive performance.
- Supports overall health: A nutritious breakfast can help provide the body with the vitamins, minerals, and nutrients it needs to function properly and support overall health.

Many successful leaders and businessmen are known to prioritize starting their day with a healthy breakfast, including:

- Elon Musk: Tesla and SpaceX CEO, is known to start his day with a simple breakfast of oatmeal or eggs.
- Richard Branson: Virgin Group founder, is a fan of a full English breakfast with eggs, bacon, and mushrooms.
- Jack Dorsey: CEO of Twitter and Square, starts his day with a light breakfast, such as fresh fruit or a smoothie.
- Tim Cook: CEO of Apple, is known to start his day with a protein-rich breakfast, such as eggs or yogurt.
- Oprah Winfrey: Media mogul, often starts her day with a protein-packed breakfast, including oatmeal with almond milk, berries, and nuts.

Food is not just fuel, it's information. It talks to your DNA and tells it what to do.

DR. BRUCE LIPTON

The food you eat can be either the
safest and most powerful form of
medicine or the slowest form of
poison.

ANN WIGMORE

A healthy breakfast is a great way to jumpstart your metabolism, fuel your body, and nourish your mind.

UNKNOWN

Breakfast is the most important meal of the day. It sets the tone for the rest of your meals and gives you the energy to tackle the day ahead.

UNKNOWN

Let food be thy medicine and
medicine be thy food.

HIPPOCRATES

Eat breakfast like a king, lunch like a prince, and dinner like a pauper.

ADELLE DAVIS

Working with your soul

Working to fulfill one's soul can be a deeply fulfilling and satisfying experience. It's important to find work that aligns with your values and interests, as this can help ensure that work is fulfilling and satisfying. It's also important to strive for work-life balance, so that work doesn't become all-consuming and negatively impact other aspects of life.

Here are a few ways in which work can help fulfill your soul:

- Sense of purpose: Work can provide a sense of purpose and meaning in life, helping individuals feel like they are making a difference and contributing to society.
- Personal growth: Work can provide opportunities for personal growth, learning, and development, which can help individuals feel more fulfilled and satisfied with their lives.
- Sense of accomplishment: Accomplishing work tasks and achieving goals can provide a sense of accomplishment and boost self-esteem, which can help individuals feel more fulfilled and satisfied with their lives.
- Connections with others: Work can provide opportunities for individuals to connect with others, form relationships, and be part of a community. These social connections can be deeply fulfilling and satisfying.
- Financial stability: Work can provide financial stability, which can help individuals feel more secure and fulfilled in their lives.

The future depends on what we do in the present.

MAH AT MA G AN D H I

Work hard in silence, let success make the noise.

UNKNOWN

Successful and unsuccessful people do not vary greatly in their abilities. They vary in their desires to reach their potential.

JO H N MAX WE L L

Your work is going to fill a large part of your life, and the only way to be truly satisfied is to do what you believe is great work. And the only way to do great work is to love what you do.

STEVE JOBS

Successful people do what
unsuccessful people are not willing to
do. Don't wish it were easier; wish
you were better.

JIM ROHN

Opportunities are usually disguised as hard work, so most people don't recognize them.

ANN LANDERS

Good relationships with coworkers

Valuing coworkers means treating them with respect, understanding, and consideration. It involves recognizing their contributions, appreciating their unique skills and perspectives, and working collaboratively to achieve common goals. Valuing coworkers also means recognizing and addressing any conflicts or challenges in a positive and constructive manner.

Valuing coworkers creates a positive work environment and can lead to increased job satisfaction, improved communication, and better collaboration and teamwork. By valuing coworkers, we can foster a culture of respect, trust, and cooperation that benefits everyone in the workplace.

Maintaining good relationships with coworkers and superiors is important for several reasons:

- Improved work environment: A positive work environment can lead to increased job satisfaction and motivation, and a more productive and efficient workplace.
- Better communication: Good relationships with coworkers and superiors can facilitate open and effective communication, leading to a better understanding of expectations and responsibilities.
- Collaboration and teamwork: Good relationships with coworkers can foster a collaborative and supportive work environment, enabling teams to work together effectively to achieve common goals.
- Career advancement: Good relationships with superiors can help facilitate career advancement opportunities and provide access to valuable mentorship and networking opportunities.
- Stress reduction: A positive work environment can reduce stress and improve overall well-being, leading to improved mental health and increased job satisfaction.

Respect your fellow human being, treat them fairly, disagree with them honestly, enjoy their friendship, explore your thoughts about one another candidly, work together for a common goal and help one another achieve it.

RICHARD M. DEVOS

The greatest compliment you can give
to someone is to believe in them and
their abilities.

UNKNOWN

You don't have to like everyone, but
you have to respect everyone.

UNKNOWN

No one can make you feel inferior without your consent.

ELEANOR ROOSEVELT

The way we communicate with others
and with ourselves ultimately
determines the quality of our lives.

TONYROBBINS

The greatest gift you can give someone is the purity of your attention.

R I CH AR D MO S S

The best way to find yourself is to
lose yourself in the service of others.

MAH AT MA G AN D H I

Working with integrity

Working with integrity means to act in accordance with moral and ethical principles, even when faced with challenging circumstances. It involves being honest, transparent, and consistent in one's actions, decisions, and communication with others.

Working with integrity also means taking responsibility for one's mistakes, striving for fairness and justice, and treating others with respect and dignity. It helps build trust and credibility, and contributes to a positive work environment and professional reputation.

Ultimately, working with integrity is about aligning one's actions with one's values, and making choices that reflect a commitment to doing what is right and just. It is an essential aspect of personal and professional growth and success.

Working with integrity in the workplace include:
- Honesty: Being truthful in your dealings with others, whether it be in reporting your work, communicating with coworkers, or representing your organization to clients.
- Ethical behavior: Acting in accordance with ethical principles, such as avoiding conflicts of interest, respecting others' intellectual property, and refraining from engaging in dishonest or illegal activities.
- Transparency: Being open and transparent in your communication and decision-making, and taking responsibility for your actions and decisions.
- Fair treatment: Treating all coworkers and clients equally, without discrimination or bias, and striving for fairness in all dealings.
- Responsibility: Taking responsibility for your mistakes, and making amends when necessary.
- Confidentiality: Keeping confidential information secure, and respecting the privacy of others.
- Respect for others: Treating others with respect, empathy, and understanding, regardless of their background or position.

Integrity is doing the right thing,
even when no one is watching.

The strength of a nation derives from
the integrity of the home.

It is not what we do once in a while that shapes our lives, but what we do consistently.

TONYROBBINS

Integrity is not a conditional word. It doesn't blow in the wind or change with the weather. It is your inner image of yourself, and if you look in there and see a man who won't cheat, then you know he never will.

JO H N D . MACD O N AL D

A man is but the product of his thoughts. What he thinks, he becomes.

MAH AT MA G AN D H I

The greatest gift you can give
someone is the purity of your
attention.

RICHARD MOSS

e some ways in which time discipline can help
this:

itization: By setting priorities and focusing on what
st important, you can ensure that your time is being
on tasks and activities that will bring the greatest
s.
ved focus: By avoiding distractions and focusing on
sk at a time, you can work more efficiently and
ely, leading to higher quality work.
lanning: With time discipline, you can plan your
week in advance, ensuring that you have enough
complete all of your tasks and meet your
ns.
stress: By being in control of their time, you can
ress and anxiety, and avoid feeling overwhelmed

productivity: By making the most of your time
ng on what is important, you can be more
get more done in less time, and achieve your
quickly.
-life balance: With time discipline, you can
you have enough time for both work and
rsuits, leading to a more balanced and

If you want to live a happy life, tie it
to a goal, not to people or things.

ALBERT EINSTEIN

Time discipline to achieve great quality

Time discipline means being in c
of time and making conscious
choices about how to allocate i
priorities, making a plan, and
schedule in order to achieve
obligations.

Time discipline also means avoi
procrastination, and focusing c
the moment. It involves being
spent, and making adjustmen
is being used effectively and

Having time discipline can
productive, reduce stress,
balance. It allows them to
make the most of their ti
and success in both thei
Time discipline is crucia
one's work and life.

Here a
achieve

- Prior
  is mo
  spent
  result
- Impro
  one ta
  effecti
- Better
  day and
  time to
  obligatic
- Reduced
  reduce st
  or rushed
- Increased
  and focus
  productive
  goals more
- Better work
  ensure that
  personal pu
  fulfilling life.

Time is a created thing. To say 'I don't have time', is like saying, 'I don't want to'.

LAO TZU

Time flies over us, but leaves its
shadow behind.

NATHANIEL HAWTHORNE

Lost time is never found again.

BENJAMIN FRANKLIN

The two most powerful warriors are patience and time.

LEOTOLSTOY

Time and tide wait for no man.

GEOFFREY CHAUCER

You may delay, but time will not.

BENJAMIN FRANKLIN

Time flies whether you're having fun
or not.

UNKNOWN

Time is precious. Use it wisely.

UNKNOWN

Take a rest if you are tired

If you are feeling exhausted or burnt out from your work, it's important to take a break and recharge in order to maintain your well-being and avoid burnout. Taking time to rest and recharge can help you be more productive and effective in the long run. It's important to prioritize self-care and listen to your body when it needs rest.

Here are some steps you can take to ensure that you get the rest you need:

- Take a break: Step away from your work or activities for a short time and give yourself a chance to rest.
- Get some fresh air: Take a walk outside or open a window to get some fresh air.
- Relax your mind: Engage in activities that you enjoy and help you relax, such as reading a book, listening to music, or practicing meditation or yoga.
- Get some exercise: Light exercise can help boost your energy levels and improve your mood.
- Get some sleep: Try to get some sleep or take a nap if possible. A good night's sleep can help you feel refreshed and recharged.
- Eat well: Make sure to eat nutritious and healthy foods that will provide you with the energy you need.
- Avoid stimulants: Avoid caffeine and other stimulants, as they can make you feel more tired in the long run.

Rest when you're weary. Refresh and renew yourself, your body, your mind, your spirit. Then get back to work.

RALPH MARSTON

Take rest; a field that has rested
gives a bountiful crop.

OVID

Rest is not idleness, and to lie
sometimes on the grass under the
trees on a summer's day, listening to
the murmur of water, or watching the
clouds float across the sky, is by no
means a waste of time.

JOHN LUBBOCK

Rest is a weapon when you're overworked and exhausted. It's a necessity, not a luxury.

BRENDON BURCHARD

Rest when you're weary. Refresh and
renew yourself, your body, your mind,
your spirit. Then get back to work.

RALPH MARSTON

Taking time to rest isn't lazy. It's necessary for your well-being and productivity.

UNKNOWN

Finish what you started

Completing our work and responsibilities is important because it demonstrates our commitment and accountability. By fulfilling our obligations, we build trust and credibility with those around us, both in our personal and professional lives.

Additionally, completing our work and responsibilities helps us to stay organized, achieve our goals, and feel a sense of accomplishment and satisfaction. When we leave tasks unfinished or neglect our responsibilities, it can lead to stress, confusion, and a lack of progress. Therefore, it is important to prioritize and manage our time effectively, so that we can successfully complete our work and responsibilities and live a more fulfilling life.

Here are some tips for managing work to finish in time:
- Prioritize tasks: Make a to-do list and prioritize tasks based on their level of urgency and importance. Tackle the most important and pressing tasks first.
- ·Set achievable goals: Break down large tasks into smaller, more manageable goals, and set deadlines for each step.
- Use time-management techniques: Experiment with different time-management techniques, such as the Pomodoro method or time blocking, to help you focus and stay on track.
- Eliminate distractions: Identify the sources of distraction in your work environment and take steps to minimize or eliminate them.
- Stay organized: Keep your work area organized, so that you can quickly find the tools and resources you need to get your work done.
- Delegate tasks: If you have too much work to handle, consider delegating some tasks to others.
- Take breaks: Regular breaks can help you avoid burnout, improve your focus, and boost your creativity and productivity.

Your work is going to fill a large part of your life, and the only way to be truly satisfied is to do what you believe is great work. And the only way to do great work is to love what you do.

STEVE JOBS

Success is not final, failure is not
fatal: it is the courage to continue
that counts.

WINSTON CHURCHILL

Successful and unsuccessful people do
not vary greatly in their abilities.
They vary in their desires to reach
their potential.

JO H N MAX WE L L

Successful people do what
unsuccessful people are not willing to
do. Don't wish it were easier; wish
you were better.

JIMROHN

The only way to do great work is to
love what you do.

STEVE JOBS

Successful people are not gifted; they just work hard, then succeed on purpose.

G.K.NIELSON

Success is not how high you have climbed, but how you make a positive difference to the world.

ROYT.BENNETT

Time with family is precious

Family is one of the most important sources of support, love, and comfort in our lives, and spending quality time with loved ones can have a positive impact on our overall well-being and happiness.

In today's fast-paced world, it can be easy to get caught up in work, daily responsibilities, and other distractions, but taking time to connect with family can help us slow down, recharge, and appreciate the things that matter most. Whether it's sharing a meal, playing a game, or just talking, spending time with family is an investment in our relationships and our own well-being, making it truly precious.

Follow these tips to create and maintain quality time with your family, building strong and lasting relationships that bring happiness and joy to your life:

- Set aside dedicated time: Make time for your family a priority and schedule it into your weekly or monthly routine.
- Unplug from technology: Turn off your phones, laptops, and other devices during family time to minimize distractions.
- Engage in activities that everyone enjoys: Choose activities that everyone in your family can participate in and enjoy, such as playing games, watching movies, or going on walks.
- Plan special experiences: Set aside time for special experiences, like family vacations, picnics, or outings to the park, that bring your family together and create lasting memories.
- Foster open communication: Encourage open and honest communication within your family. This can be done through family meetings, one-on-one conversations, or just casual chats during meals.
- Show appreciation: Take time to express your gratitude and appreciation for each member of your family. A simple compliment or kind word can go a long way in fostering positive relationships.

The love of a family is life's greatest blessing.

UNKNOWN

Family is not an important thing. It's everything.

MICHAEL J. FOX

The family is one of nature's masterpieces.

GEORGE SANTAYANA

A happy family is but an earlier
heaven.

GEORGE BERNARD SHAW

Together we make a family.

The family is the first essential cell of
human society.

POPE JOHN XXIII

Family is the source of the strongest and most meaningful relationships in our lives.

UNKNOWN

The family is the test of freedom;
because the family is the only thing
that the free man makes for himself
and by himself.

GILBERT K. CHESTERTON

There's no place like home.

L . F R A N K B A U M

The love of a family is life's greatest gift.

UNKNOWN

The power of prayer

The power of prayer is a concept that is central to many religious beliefs. According to these beliefs, prayer is a way for individuals to connect with a higher power and request help, guidance, or blessings.

For many people, prayer can be a source of comfort, strength, and hope. Some research has suggested that prayer may have a positive impact on physical and mental health, although more research is needed to fully understand this relationship. Additionally, prayer can serve as a way for individuals to express gratitude and reflect on their values and beliefs. Ultimately, the power of prayer is a deeply personal and subjective experience that is unique to each individual.

Prayer is not asking. It is a longing of the soul. It is daily admission of one's weakness. It is better in prayer to have a heart without words than words without a heart.

MAH AT MA G AN D H I

Prayer is not asking God for things; it is laying hold of God's promises. Prayer is not a matter of asking God to do something for us; it is a matter of God doing something with us.

K.P. YOHANNAN

Prayer is like a telephone, only you don't have to pay for the call. All you have to do is to lift the receiver and God will do the rest.

CORRIE TENBOOM

Prayer is when you talk to God;
meditation is when you listen to God.

DIANA ROBINSON

The power of prayer is not in the words we say, but in the faith we put into them.

ANONYMOUS

Prayer is the key that unlocks all the storehouses of God's infinite grace and power.

R.A. TORREY

Prayer is not just asking God for things; it's also about listening to what God is saying to you.

R I CK WAR R E N

Prayer is not asking God to do
something for you; it's asking God to
do something with you.

WILLIAM PAUL YOUNG

Prayer is the breath of the soul. It is
the secret of spiritual power.

R.A. TORREY

Prayer is not a mysterious practice reserved only for clergy and the religiously devout. Prayer is simply communicating with God—listening and talking to him. People of all faiths, even those with no faith at all, can benefit from prayer.

BILLY GRAHAM

Deep sleep is the best medicine

Getting adequate and quality sleep can be beneficial for one's physical and mental health. Sleep is important for the body to restore and rejuvenate itself, and it also has a significant impact on one's overall well-being.

Lack of sleep can lead to various health problems and affect mood, memory, and cognitive function. On the other hand, getting enough sleep can help improve focus, boost the immune system, and reduce the risk of various health conditions. It is recommended that adults get 7-9 hours of sleep per night, although the exact amount may vary for each individual based on their needs and schedule.

Sleep is the best meditation.

D AL AI L AMA

Sleep is the golden chain that ties health and our bodies together.

THOMAS DEKKER

A good night's sleep is one of life's great pleasures.

MAR CI A CR O S S

The night is a gift, as is sleep. Enjoy both.

JIM BUTCHER

Sleep is the best way to recharge your batteries, refresh your mind and restore your spirit.

Deep sleep is like a resurrection, a washing of the soul.

TERRYPRATCHETT

A good night's sleep is a pillar of good health.

CHINESEPROVERB

A rested body is a happy body.

UNKNOWN

The best sleep is the sleep you dream of.

UNKNOWN

Good sleep, deep sleep, peaceful sleep, is like a balm to the soul.

ANNE MORROW LINDBERGH

9 7 9 8 3 7 6 9 0 7 6 0 3